Robert Parris Moses

by Bianca Dumas

Chicago, Illinois

For information, address the publisher:
Raintree, 100 N. LaSalle, Suite 1200, Chicago, IL 60602

Printed and bound in the United States at Lake Book Manufacturing, Inc.
07 06 05 04 03
10 9 8 7 6 5 4 3 2 1

Library of Congress Cataloging-in-Publication Data:

Dumas, Bianca.
  Robert Moses / Bianca Dumas.
    v. cm. -- (African-American biographies)
Includes bibliographical references and index.
Contents: The early years -- Helping others -- Helping people vote --
The work gets harder -- Freedom summer -- A new party -- A new kind of
civil rights work -- Time line.
  ISBN 0-7398-7031-9 (library binding-hardcover) -- ISBN 1-4109-0319-2
(pbk.)
  1. Moses, Robert Parris--Juvenile literature. 2. African American
civil rights workers--Mississippi--Biography--Juvenile literature. 3.
Civil rights workers--Mississippi--Biography--Juvenile literature. 4.
African Americans--Civil rights--Mississippi--History--20th
century--Juvenile literature. 5. Civil rights
movements--Mississippi--History--20th century--Juvenile literature. 6.
Mississippi--Race relations--Juvenile literature. 7. African American
teachers--Biography--Juvenile literature. 8. Mathematics--Study and
teaching--History--20th century--Juvenile literature. [1. Moses, Robert
Parris. 2. Civil rights workers. 3. African Americans--Biography.] I.
Title. II. Series.
  E185.97.M89D86 2004
  323'.092--dc21

                          2003002199

Acknowledgments
The publisher would like to thank the following for permission to reproduce photographs:
pp. 4, 8, 31, 38, 46 George Ballis/Take Stock; pp. 6, 10, 14, 17, 26, 34, 37. 40, 43, 51, 52 Bettmann/Corbis; p. 12
Library of Congress; pp. 20, 28 Matt Herron/Take Stock; p. 24 Flip Schulke/Corbis; pp. 48, 58 Associated Press, AP;
p. 55 Getty Images; p. 57 Reuters NewMedia Inc./Corbis.

Cover Photograph: Associated Press, AP

Every effort has been made to contact copyright holders of any material reproduced in this book. Any omissions will
be rectified in subsequent printings if notice is given to the publisher.

Some words are shown in bold, **like this.** You can find out what
they mean by looking in the glossary.

Contents

Robert Moses fought for the rights of African Americans. In 1964 he attended the Democratic National Convention to help get black Americans represented in politics.

Introduction

Robert Parris Moses was an important leader in the **Civil Rights** **Movement** of the 1960s. The Civil Rights Movement fought for all people to receive the same freedoms and treatment under the law. People in this movement worked hard to win **equal rights** for African Americans. Equal rights are when people have the same opportunities and are treated the same, no matter what their race or gender.

Robert did not become as famous as some other leaders of the time. This was because he did not want to be in the public eye. He did not want to be on television or give speeches to thousands of people. Instead, he worked behind the scenes of the Civil Rights Movement. He planned events and taught other people how to be leaders.

The work Robert did was hard and dangerous. He traveled to the South to help African Americans have better lives. Some white people there did not want Robert to help. At that time, there was a

An African-American man spells out the word "vote" on his forehead in 1965. Robert fought hard to register black people to vote during the Civil Rights Era.

lot of **discrimination** in the South. Discrimination is treating people unfairly because of differences like skin color. Some white people became angry that Robert was trying to end this discrimination. Robert was beaten and put in jail several times while he was working in the South. Some white people even tried to kill him.

Robert had no real home during the years of the **Civil Rights Era** (1955–1965). He traveled around Mississippi helping African Americans. He started schools and helped African Americans sign up to vote.

After the Civil Rights Era, Robert did another important thing. He taught math. Robert's work as a teacher was a kind of civil rights work, too. He taught math to students who thought they could not learn math. Many of these students were African American. They learned math so they could go to college like Robert did.

In his own words

"You have to break off a little chunk of a problem and work on it, and try to see where it leads, and concentrate on it."

"This is my life. And I learned it in the sixties. That is, I learned that this was my life really living in a form of struggle. And I think that you can have a good life in this country in struggle. I think it's one of the few ways you can have a good life in this country."

Robert's parents always encouraged him to work hard and get a good education so that he could go far in life.

Chapter 1:
The Early Years

Robert Moses was born in Harlem, New York, on January 23, 1935. His father was a security guard at a local armory. An armory is a factory that makes weapons. His mother worked hard to take care of Robert and his brothers. His parents tried to save as much money as they could so their sons could go to good schools.

Times were tough when Robert was growing up. He was born in the middle of the **Great Depression** (1929–1939). During this time, many businesses failed and banks closed. Many people in the United States lost their jobs and their homes. Robert's father did not make much money. But he felt lucky to have a job.

When Robert was a child, he got up early in the morning to sell milk. He and his mother and brothers sold the milk for 19 cents a quart. They earned one penny on each quart they sold. Robert's family sold milk so they could afford to buy some milk

Just like these Stuyvesant students, Robert studied many subjects, including laboratory science. At the time, Robert was one of the only African Americans to attend the high school.

for themselves. They tried to sell 40 quarts of milk a day. That way, they could buy two quarts of milk for the family.

High school

Robert's parents believed a good education would help him succeed. Robert studied hard. He took a test when he was eleven years old to get into the well-known Stuyvesant High School in downtown Manhattan. Only the best students with the highest scores could attend the school. He was chosen to attend the high school.

Stuyvesant High School offered very difficult classes where one had to read, write, and study all the time. Black and white students went to the school together. Robert studied and did well. He was elected president of his class. He was also captain of the baseball team.

Robert's hard work at Stuyvesant paid off. He received a **scholarship** to attend Hamilton College. A scholarship is a grant or prize that pays for someone to go to college.

Hamilton College

Hamilton College was a private four-year college in Clinton, New York. There were only three African-American students at the college. Robert was very quiet and did well in his classes. He was co-captain of the basketball team. He was the vice president of his class.

Philosophy was one of Robert's favorite subjects. Philosophy is the study of a person's ideas and beliefs about how life should be lived. From philosophy classes, Robert came to believe that people should not allow themselves to be treated poorly. But they should not be cruel to the people who are being mean. Otherwise, they would be just as bad as the people who are treating them poorly.

Volunteering

Robert cared about other people. He wanted to help people change their lives for the better. He also wanted to learn about the world

This is Harvard University in Cambridge, Massachusetts. Robert received his master's degree in philosophy from Harvard University in 1957.

around him. During his summer breaks, he was able to travel around the world. Everywhere he went, he worked without being paid. This is called being a **volunteer.** This offered him a chance to see the world and help people at the same time. Money did not matter to him.

Robert visited Belgium, France, Germany, and Japan. He worked at a kids' summer camp in Belgium. Robert worked on a farm in Germany. He dug up potatoes so that the sick people at a hospital could have food. In Japan, he built steps so that sick children could climb the steep hill near their hospital.

Harvard

In 1956 Robert graduated from Hamilton. He was 21 years old. He decided that he wanted to continue his education and study **philosophy.** Robert applied for graduate school. In graduate school, people do advanced study of a single subject. He was accepted into the famous Harvard University in Cambridge, Massachusetts.

Robert received a master's degree in philosophy in 1957. He decided to continue working toward his doctorate degree. That is the highest degree a person can get. It usually takes at least three years to earn.

In 1958 Robert's mother became sick with cancer and died. She was only 43 years old. His father became very sad after her death. He was so sad that he was placed in a mental hospital for several months.

Robert decided to quit his studies at Harvard to take care of his father. His father was released from the hospital, and Robert moved back to New York. He took a job teaching math at Horace Mann High School. After a time his father got better and returned to work at the armory.

On February 2, 1960, college students Joseph McNeil, Franklin McCain, Billy Smith, and Clarence Henderson sat at a whites-only lunch counter in Greensboro, North Carolina, to protest segregation.

Chapter 2:
Getting Involved

In 1960 Moses read about a famous **protest** in the newspaper. A protest is when people join together to show they are against something. On February 1, 1960, four African-American college students sat at a lunch counter in Greensboro, North Carolina, that served only white people. They refused to leave until they were served. They did this to protest **segregation.** Segregation is the act of separating people because of their race. At that time, many places were only for white people. Black people often had to eat at different restaurants, go to different schools, and shop in different stores.

People who thought African Americans and whites should not eat together called the students names. Some even poured drinks on the students' heads. The students were never served. But they did not leave until the store closed for the night. This kind of protest was called a **sit-in.** African Americans went into places reserved for white people and stayed there to protest.

Robert had already helped organize a march to end segregation in New York schools. Now he wanted to go south to see the protests. In the spring of 1960, Robert visited his Uncle Bill in Virginia. There, he read about a **protest** in the local newspaper. People were protesting because the town's businesses served only white people. African Americans were not allowed in their stores.

The protest Robert read about had a **picket line.** People in picket lines march in front of the thing they are protesting. They carry signs so that people walking by can see why they dislike the thing. Robert joined the picket line. The picket line marched in front of the businesses. Robert carried a sign that said he was unhappy with their decision to serve only white people.

Later, he said that he suddenly felt very free. He had finally found a peaceful way to take action and change the world.

The Southern Christian Leadership Conference

Robert did something else life-changing during his visit to his uncle. He went to a speech given by the Reverend Wyatt Tee Walker. Walker was a member of a group called the **Southern Christian Leadership Conference (SCLC).**

Dr. Martin Luther King Jr. started the SCLC. King was a preacher and a **civil rights** leader. He believed that African Americans deserved **equal rights.** He gave speeches and planned

On May 9, 1963, Dr. Martin Luther King Jr. (seated, left), spoke at a press conference with the Reverend Ralph Abernathy in Birmingham, Alabama. Dr. King worked hard for racial equality and for peace.

peaceful protests to demand that laws be changed. Walker explained how some white people were trying to stop King from doing his work. Dr. King was arrested and sued. Walker encouraged people to help raise money to defend King.

Robert volunteered for the Committee to Defend Martin Luther King when he got back to New York. He worked at the high school during the day. At night, Robert worked doing office work, mailing letters, and raising money for the committee.

After school let out that summer, Robert went to Atlanta to work at **SCLC** headquarters. In Atlanta, Robert did office work and helped **register** people to vote. Americans have to register before they can vote. This means they have to fill out a form and answer some questions. He also went to protests whenever he could.

A new group

Ella Baker was one of the leaders of the SCLC. Robert got to know her and admired her ideas. Baker wanted to start a new group that focused on training ordinary people to be leaders in the **Civil Rights** Movement. She left the SCLC and started the **Student Nonviolent Coordinating Committee (SNCC).**

SNCC was made up mainly of of college students. The group's focus was on ending segregation in the South. They organized **nonviolent protests** and registered African-American voters. They started schools and trained people in each community to be leaders. Robert started working for SNCC, too.

In August of 1960, SNCC sent Robert to Mississippi. Mississippi was a very dangerous state for civil rights workers. Many people there practiced **discrimination** against African Americans. African Americans were sometimes beaten or even killed if they did anything the white people did not like.

Ella Baker

Ella Baker (1903–1986) became interested in civil rights as a young girl. Her grandparents had been enslaved. Her grandmother was whipped by her owner. She had refused to marry the man her owner had chosen for her.

In 1940 Baker began working for the **National Organization for the Advancement of Colored People (NAACP).** The NAACP worked to gain freedoms for African Americans. Baker helped the NAACP expand throughout the South. She helped in the fight to get rid of segregation in New York schools.

In 1957 Baker began working with the Southern Christian Leadership Conference. Baker agreed with their stand on **equal rights.** But she disagreed with the way the organization was run. She did not believe that one single person should be the leader. Instead, Baker wanted ordinary people to work for freedom themselves. Then these people could lead each other.

So, in 1960 Baker helped create a new group called Student Nonviolent Coordinating Committee (SNCC). Baker's belief in many leaders instead of just one was popular in SNCC. She was a quiet and encouraging leader at the SNCC. She was very well respected by the student members.

Baker also worked for many other civil rights groups. She kept working for freedom and equal rights until she died in 1986.

Robert speaks to a group of African Americans in a Mississippi church. A member of SNCC, he went to Mississippi in 1961 to help African Americans fight unfair practices based on race.

Chapter 3:
Helping People Vote

On the advice of Ella Baker, Robert met a man named Amzie Moore who lived in Mississippi. Moore was the president of the local chapter of the **National Association for the Advancement of Colored People (NAACP).** The NAACP is a national group that works to gain **equal rights** for African Americans. He soon became one of Robert's most important teachers.

At first, Robert wanted to lead some **protests** like the **sit-in** in North Carolina. Moore told Robert that this was a bad idea. The white people who wanted Mississippi to be **segregated** would not allow protests. They would just beat, kill, or throw protesters in jail for a long time. Moore said the best thing to do was to teach African Americans to vote.

Moore took Robert to meet the African Americans in Cleveland, Mississippi. Most of them lived in shacks. The children

Amzie Moore

Amzie Moore was born in Mississippi in 1911. He was first interested in **civil rights** when serving in the U.S. Army during World War II (1939–1945). During the war, he saw how African Americans were treated in Europe. There was no **segregation** as there was in the United States. Segregation is the separation of people according to the color of their skin. Moore began to work for civil rights when he returned home.

Moore had one of the few black-owned gas stations in Mississippi. He refused to build separate bathrooms for white and African-American people.

Moore was a local leader in the **National Association for the Advancement of Colored People (NAACP)** during the **Civil Rights Era** (1955–1965). He helped people register and encouraged them to vote. He believed that the key to African-American success was to have a voice in politics. They needed to elect people who would work to improve living conditions and educational programs.

Moore also believed that African Americans needed to have land to be successful. He believed they needed training in how to farm and take care of the land. In his later years, he helped to build good housing for poor people. He died in 1982.

ate only one meal a day and were always hungry. Then Robert understood why African Americans had to vote in Mississippi. They could have better lives if they could elect leaders who would help them.

The Mississippi government made it hard for African Americans to vote. They knew that if African Americans could not vote then there could not be change. In some places, people had |to pay a tax before they could **register.** In other places, people had to take a test. The tests were often nearly impossible for African Americans to pass. One man was told to read some words that were in Chinese. When he could not do it, he was told he could not vote. The voting rules were not legal.

Freedom School

Robert walked from house to house. He showed the people a voter registration form. He told them how important it was to vote.

Robert started a Freedom School at the town church. Freedom Schools were started in poor areas that did not have good schools for African-American children. Teachers at the Freedom School taught students about African-American history and culture. They also taught basic education and how the country's government works. At the Freedom School, Robert taught adults how to register to vote. He taught them how to fill out the form. He also taught them how to answer questions that might be on the test. Robert reminded the people that it was their civil right to vote.

Civil rights activists helped African-American voters in the South fill out the voter registration cards. Robert thought voting was important for creating change.

African Americans in other towns soon asked Robert to help them **register** to vote. More and more African Americans wanted freedom. But becoming free was dangerous work.

Going to jail

Next, Robert went to Amite County, Mississippi. No African Americans were registered to vote there. In August 1961, Robert brought three black people to the Amite County courthouse to register to vote. The man working in the courthouse made them wait six hours before he let them register.

A policeman arrested Robert when the three finally left the courthouse. Most white people in Mississippi did not want African Americans to vote. They did not like that Robert was helping black people register to vote. They wanted him to go back to New York. White people in Mississippi often made their own rules at that time. They could throw people in jail just because they wanted to.

The policeman told Robert that if he paid five dollars he could get out of jail. But he refused to pay. He said he was not in jail for a legal reason. He said he should not have to pay. In the black community at that time, going to jail as a **protester** was a noble thing to do. It was not viewed as criminal behavior.

Robert was allowed one call before he was put into the jail cell. He shocked the police with his call. He called the Justice Department in Washington, D.C. Robert told them what happened. He told them that he was not in jail for a legal reason. He said that other black people were being treated unfairly as well. Robert asked the Justice Department to investigate the problems in Mississippi.

Robert stayed in jail for two days. Then a lawyer visited him. He paid the bail money, and Robert got out of jail. But Robert went right back to work trying to register more black voters.

In the 1950s and 1960s, it was dangerous for African Americans to register to vote. In 1966, Tom Flowers, a 68-year-old man, risked registering at the county courthouse in Batesville, Mississippi.

A week later, Robert brought two more men to the courthouse to register. This time three white men were waiting outside. They stopped Robert when he tried to enter. One man hit Robert on the head with the handle of a knife. The other men kicked him. He practiced his peaceful **philosophy** and did not fight back. When he stood up, he said he was still going in to the courthouse. There, Robert told a police officer what had happened. But the officer did not do anything about the beating.

High school students protest

Every day, more African Americans joined the **Civil Rights**
Movement. In McComb, Mississippi, two high school students
held a **sit-in** at the bus station. They were arrested. They were
finally released after a month in jail. But their principal would not
let them come back to school. The students at the school got angry.
In October 1961, about 100 of them marched out of school.

The students marched to the **SNCC** office. They asked Robert
and the SNCC volunteers for help. Then they all held a **protest** at
the city hall. They knelt down to pray on the steps of the building.
Police arrested everyone. Robert stayed in jail for three days.

The students could only go back to school if they promised that
they would not protest anymore. They were also given lower grades
in their classes. More than 100 students walked out of the school
again. They refused to make the promise or accept the lower grades.

Robert and the SNCC opened a school for these students. It
was called **Nonviolent** High School. The school was another way to
protest without fighting. The local judge soon closed the school. The
police sent Robert to jail again. This time, he stayed in jail for 39 days.

Robert and fellow civil rights worker, Mendy Samstein, take calls at the SNCC office. The work of the organization was so dangerous that SNCC workers out on a job were required to call the office frequently to let the others know they were ok.

Chapter 4:
The Work Gets Harder

White people in Mississippi were becoming very angry with all of the **protests** and **civil rights** work. They did not want African Americans to protest or to **register** to vote. The government of Mississippi decided to punish the people.

Many African Americans in Mississippi were poor. They needed help from the government to survive. In summer, they often grew and ate their own crops. During the winter, the government passed out small amounts of free food. But in the winter of 1963, the government did not pass out the free food. People were not prepared, and they did not have the money to buy food. One baby starved to death and many people got sick.

The **SNCC** workers were furious. They told people all around the United States what had happened. People in other states sent food to the African Americans in Mississippi. The support from people in other places made some whites even angrier. They bombed four African-American businesses. The businesses burned down because of the bombs.

A shooting

One night, three white men sat in a car outside the **SNCC** office. Robert and two volunteers left the office and got into their car. A volunteer named Jimmy Travis drove. The white men pulled alongside the SNCC car. One of them pointed a machine gun out the window and started shooting at the car.

One of the bullets hit Travis in the shoulder. They rushed Travis to the hospital. It was amazing that Travis lived and recovered. It was also amazing that nobody else was shot. There were thirteen bullet holes in the car.

People think the men meant to shoot Robert. Many people blamed Robert because African Americans in Mississippi now wanted **civil rights.** The three men were never found or arrested for their crime.

Telling Washington

On May 8, 1963, Robert raced to a burning house. The owner of the house was an African-American farmer named Hartman Turnbow. White men bombed and burned Turnbow's house because he tried to **register** to vote. The men also tried to kill

Robert Moses was becoming a well-known civil rights activist. Although he tried to stay behind the scenes, he was often recognized and was occasionally the target of violent attacks.

Turnbow. They tried to keep him inside the house while it burned. But Turnbow shot at the men and was able to get out of the house.

The sheriff arrived and arrested Hartman Turnbow and Robert. The sheriff told the local newspaper that Turnbow bombed his own house. He said Turnbow wanted to blame whites for the bombing. Robert and Turnbow were kept in jail for several days.

Robert went to Washington, D.C., after he was released from jail. He told government officials how dangerous Mississippi was for African Americans. But there was not a single government official who would promise to help him.

A sad event made some white people begin to listen. On June 7, 1963, a well-known **civil rights** leader named Medgar Evers was shot and killed. Medgar was a field leader with the **NAACP.** He had **protested** and gave many speeches encouraging people to vote.

People all around North America heard about this murder. African Americans got angrier and held more protests. Many more white people got involved in the fight for civil rights and joined the protests. These things made the voter **registration** project stronger.

The Freedom Vote

Some white people in Mississippi said African Americans were free and did not vote because they did not want to. Robert and the other civil rights workers knew this was not true. African Americans did not vote because it was hard and dangerous to register.

Robert helped create the Freedom Vote in 1963. This was a mock, or pretend, election. Eighty thousand African Americans in Mississippi voted in the mock election. The votes in the mock election did not count. But the votes showed that African Americans wanted to vote in real elections. The white people were wrong.

Medgar Evers

Medgar Evers (1925–1963) was born in Decatur, Mississippi. Since he was a young boy, Evers did not like how badly white people treated black people. He wanted to find a better life for himself. He could have moved north, where life was easier for African Americans. Instead, Evers decided to help people in Mississippi achieve **equal rights**.

After college, Evers sold insurance to African Americans. When Evers worked, he saw how poor African American farmers were treated unfairly. He wanted to help them. He decided that he would become a lawyer and represent these people in court. At that time, law schools in Mississippi only accepted white people. That did not stop Evers. He became the first African American to apply to a law school in Mississippi. The school would not let him in. So Evers tried a different way to help African Americans.

In 1954 Evers went to work for the National Association for the Advancement of Colored People (NAACP). He gave speeches about civil rights and helped African Americans to vote. He worked to end segregation in Mississippi's schools. Evers helped African Americans fight against unfair treatment and organized protests. Slowly, things began to change. But not everyone was happy with the changes.

Byron De La Beckwith was a white man who did not want equal rights for African Americans. He shot and killed Evers in 1963. In 1994 Beckwith was finally convicted and jailed for killing Evers.

Fighting for equal rights was becoming more and more dangerous. At this 1964 sit-in in an Annapolis, Maryland, restaurant, a police officer arrests an African-American protester.

Chapter 5:
Freedom Summer

People began to call Robert and the **SNCC civil rights** workers Freedom Fighters. The Freedom Fighters wanted thousands of African Americans to **register** to vote for the real elections. So they created the 1964 project, Freedom Summer.

In Ohio, 1,000 college students gathered to learn about the project. Most of the students were white. SNCC member James Forten spoke to the students in Ohio. He spoke slowly and quietly, and everybody listened. Forten warned the students that Mississippi was a dangerous place. He told them they might be killed there. It was dangerous to try to help African Americans register to vote in Mississippi.

Forten told the **volunteers** that they were not allowed to carry guns. They could not fight back if anyone attacked them. The volunteers had to practice **nonviolence,** even in the dangerous

South. Many **volunteers** would go to jail. Forten hoped that others would see how much the volunteers believed in their cause. Maybe then, people would begin to change their minds.

On June 21 the first group of volunteers left for Mississippi. By the next day, three volunteers were already missing. No one knew what had happened. Police officers in Mississippi said the men were hiding to gain attention to the project. It was soon learned that the three volunteers were dead.

Teaching the people

Some volunteers started more Freedom Schools in places where there were not any schools. Teachers there taught English, African-American history, and other subjects to African-American children. They also taught people how to **register** to vote. Some volunteers worked at Freedom Clinics. These were health-care centers started in poor places with no medical care. African Americans and volunteers could visit the doctor at these Freedom Clinics.

Robert met a Freedom Fighter named Donna Richards. She taught in Freedom Schools and helped African Americans register to vote. Donna and Robert both shared the same ideas. They believed in the same causes. They fell in love and got married.

Life was becoming more dangerous every day. White people bombed churches and beat up the volunteers on the street. Robert

Freedom Schools, such as this one in Cleveland, Ohio, were started as an alternative to the public schools. These schools were opened so that all African Americans could receive a good public education.

Robert was a brave man who refused to back down in the face of danger. He was willing to risk his life for his beliefs.

said that he had to learn to live with fear. He said he sometimes had to tell himself to lift up his feet and start walking. He was so afraid that he could think only of taking one step at a time.

Robert takes a nap

Robert was known for his tranquility. Tranquility is calmness and peacefulness. The **SNCC** volunteers counted on Robert to be tranquil even in scary times.

One night, men with guns broke into the SNCC office. They kicked down the door and flipped over the table and chairs. They stole important papers. The **volunteers** in the office were able to escape right before the burglary. The men probably would have killed the volunteers.

Robert and a friend came to check on the building just a few hours later. They found the mess inside. Robert's friend was scared. But Robert laid a blanket on the couch in the office. He planned to go to sleep right there.

This story became very famous. It was an example of Robert's courage. People who worked with Robert thought he was like a character in a storybook. He seemed strong and completely fearless. Many volunteers wanted to be like him. Robert was an inspiration for many people, both black and white.

Robert knew that Freedom Fighters would not be at risk if they had not come to Mississippi. Fighting for equality was important work but it was also dangerous. Robert said that he never asked volunteers to do work that he would not do. He thought the work so important that he was willing to risk his life.

In August 1964, members of the Mississippi Freedom Party form a circle and hold hands outside of the convention center where the Democratic National Convention was being held in New Jersey.

Chapter 6:
A New Party

Some African Americans visited the yearly meeting of the Democratic Party in Mississippi in the summer of 1964. The Democratic Party is one of two main groups that help run the U.S. government. They met to discuss new laws and elect new leaders.

The leaders of the Democratic Party were unhappy. They did not want African Americans to go to the meetings. African Americans would change Mississippi if they could change the laws and leaders. Democrats wanted to keep Mississippi the way it was.

The party leaders did their best to keep African Americans out of the meetings. Sometimes they moved the meetings without telling the black people. Other times they canceled the meetings so the African Americans could not attend.

Gathering together

Robert and the **SNCC volunteers** had an idea. In August 1964, they created their own **Democratic Party.** They called this the Mississippi Freedom Democratic Party. It was also known as the Freedom Party. They held their own meetings.

Poor African-American farmers came to the meetings. They learned to talk about their ideas. Many learned to speak in front of a crowd. This was the first time anyone had listened to the farmers' ideas.

Even people who had almost been killed came to the meetings. E.W. Steptoe was a brave **civil rights** worker whose actions had endangered the lives of himself and his family. Turnbow's home was burned down when he tried to **register** to vote. But they both came to the meetings. They wanted civil rights so much that they could not be scared away.

A trip to New Jersey

The Freedom Party elected 68 people to go to the Democratic Party's national **convention** in New Jersey. National conventions are held once every four years. At the conventions, members of the political parties pick a candidate for president. The conventions last several days. At convention meetings, people give speeches. They vote to decide what leaders, ideas, and laws they want to support.

On August 24, 1964, civil rights activists held an all-night protest calling for the right of the Mississippi Freedom Party to be seated at the Democratic National Convention.

Members of the Freedom Party wanted to talk to U.S. President Lyndon Johnson. They wanted to tell him how black people were treated in Mississippi. They wanted to tell him that they were not allowed to attend meetings of the Democratic Party.

The Freedom Party hoped the President would understand. Then he could tell the regular Democrats from Mississippi to leave the convention because they broke the law. It was illegal not to allow African Americans to attend the meetings. The Freedom Party would then be able to replace the regular democrats at the convention.

Dr. Martin Luther King Jr.

Baptist minister Dr. Martin Luther King Jr. (1929-1968) was a leader of the **Civil Rights** Movement. The Civil Rights Movement was the actions taken to gain fair and **equal rights** for African Americans between 1955 and 1965. He was the head of the Southern Christian Leaders Conference. Like Robert Parris Moses, King believed in **nonviolence.** He tried to find peaceful ways to gain civil rights for all Americans.

Dr. King was born in Georgia in 1929. He was an excellent speaker and gave many inspiring speeches. King also led many marches and protests in the 1960s. He led a huge march in Washington, D.C., in 1963. There, he gave his famous "I Have a Dream" speech. King said his dream was for his small children to grow up in a land of freedom. He wanted all people, black and white, to be treated equally. In 1964 King was awarded the Nobel Peace Prize. King also helped to get the Voting Rights Act of 1965 passed in Congress. This made it illegal to deny people the right to vote because of the color of their skin.

Dr. King's work encouraged many African Americans and whites to work for civil rights. But his work angered others. On April 4, 1968, King was shot to death in Memphis, Tennessee. James Earl Ray was sentenced to 99 years in prison for the murder. Today, the nation honors King on the third Monday in January. This national holiday is called Martin Luther King Jr. Day.

Robert Moses was one of the strongest leaders of the Freedom Party. He went to New Jersey with Steptoe, Turnbow, and the others. Martin Luther King Jr. also went to New Jersey. By this time, King was a famous black leader and speaker. These leaders all wanted the opinions and concerns of the African-American people to be heard.

A Mississippi woman named Fannie Lou Hamer spoke at the **convention.** She told a story about her life. One day Hamer was arrested during a **protest.** The white police officer put her in a jail cell with some male prisoners. He told the other prisoners to beat Hamer. They beat her until she screamed. She was hurt so badly that she could not walk back to her own jail cell. Hamer's speech was played on national TV. People all around the country were sad to hear her story. They sent messages to President Johnson that night. They told him to let the Freedom Party stay.

The Freedom Party loses

Members of the Mississippi **Democratic Party** were furious. They said they would leave the convention if the Freedom Party were allowed to stay. Members of the Democratic Parties from Arkansas and Louisiana said they would leave, too. This became a problem for President Johnson. He needed people to vote for him in the upcoming election. People from those states might not vote for him if their party members left.

Robert explains the Mississippi Freedom Party's position to the press from the floor of the Democratic National Convention. People had given their convention passes to MFP members so they could get in.

Democratic Party leaders, Martin Luther King Jr. and President Johnson agreed that two members of the Freedom Party could stay at the **convention,** but they could not vote. Robert and other members of the Freedom Party including Fannie Lou Hamer said no. But the president went on television and said that they had accepted the plan.

Robert knew this was unfair. That night, the members of the Freedom Party tried to join the convention anyway. They sat in some empty seats until the police made some of them move. The next night Robert and some **SNCC volunteers** went to the convention. They stood outside in a **picket line.**

Although the Freedom Party was not able to participate at the convention, they did have some success. People all around the nation became interested in **civil rights** after they saw the Freedom Party on TV. Supporting civil rights became very popular among black and white people across the country. This new popularity in civil rights brought about changes. In 1964 Congress passed the 24th Amendment. An amendment is a change that is made to a law or legal document. This amendment to the Constitution made it illegal to charge people a tax to vote. More African Americans were able to **register** to vote after this law was passed.

On July 2, 1964, President Johnson signed the Civil Rights Act of 1964. This law gave the U.S. government power to stop **discrimination** in public places. Bosses who did not hire people just because of their skin color could go to jail. State programs that practiced discrimination could not receive any money from the national government.

On August 6, 1965, President Johnson signed the Voting Rights Act. This law made reading tests for voters illegal.

Robert Moses, shown here in a July 19, 2000 photo, may not have been the best-known leader in the Civil Rights Movement. But his hard work and dedication have made a huge difference.

Chapter 7:
A New Kind of Civil Rights Work

Robert kept working for **civil rights.** But his type of work changed. He traveled to other countries as he did in college. He felt that the Civil Rights Movement in the United States was only part of a larger mission. He wanted to work for peaceful change in many places around the world.

Robert's first visit to Africa was in September 1964. Some other civil rights workers went on the trip with him. They told African leaders about the difficult lives of African Americans.

Robert makes changes

Robert and his wife Donna decided to leave Mississippi when Freedom Summer ended. In 1965 he changed his name to Robert Parris. He felt that too many people recognized his name. He thought that he was becoming too famous for his work in Mississippi. Instead, he wanted people to pay attention to some of the new leaders. He wanted other young people to become leaders, too. This was Ella Baker's **philosophy**. Robert still thought this was the best way to work.

One of the changes Robert wanted to work toward was the end of the Vietnam War (1954–1975). American soldiers had been fighting the spread of communism from North Vietnam into South Vietnam. Communism is a way of organizing a country's markets. In a communist country, everything belongs to the government, and everyone shares the profits. The American government did not like communism. They thought communist countries did not allow their people enough freedom. But not all Americans thought their country should be involved in the war.

Robert and other African Americans began to **protest** the war. They wanted peace in the world. They also protested the draft. Many men were drafted, or made to serve in the U.S. army, during the Vietnam War. All young men who were eighteen and older had to **register** for the draft. Hundreds of thousands of young men were sent to war. But many of them went because they were drafted. They did not choose to sign up for the army.

The draft made many African Americans angry. They did not want to be forced to fight for freedom in another country. They felt that African Americans were not yet completely free in America.

Many people protested the Vietnam War. In March of 1966, the world-famous boxer and war protester Muhammad Ali pointed to a headline that showed he was not the only one against the conflict.

This was a tiring time for Robert. His never-ending work had put a strain on his marriage. He and his wife, Donna, divorced in 1966.

A move to Africa

Robert did not believe in the Vietnam War. He would not register for the draft. But it was illegal not to register. People who did not register could be put in jail. So he went to Canada to live. There he met Janet. She had also been a freedom fighter during Freedom Summer. They fell in love and were married.

President Jimmy Carter spoke with reporters after a press conference in March 1977. As president, Carter pardoned all persons who had avoided the draft for the Vietnam War.

Robert and Janet decided to leave Canada. In 1968, they moved to Tanzania, a country in east Africa. In Tanzania, he and his wife worked in a school. Robert taught math and his wife taught English.

Robert rested while he was in Africa. He thought about the lessons he had learned while working for **civil rights.** He thought about the risks he had taken.

He and Janet were in Africa for about eight years. There, they had four children—daughters Maisha and Malaika and sons Omowale and Tabasuri.

Then, U.S. President Jimmy Carter granted a pardon. A pardon forgives or excuses someone for his or her actions. Carter pardoned everyone who had refused to **register** for the draft or be drafted. These people could return to the United States again. They would not be put in jail. In 1976 Robert and his family moved to Cambridge, Massachusetts.

Robert goes back to school

Robert Moses finally got the chance to return to Harvard to earn his doctorate degree. He was a now a doctor of **philosophy.** His wife became a children's doctor. But Robert and Janet were still civil rights workers at heart. Robert found a new way he wanted to help African Americans. He decided that the new issue facing African Americans was poor education. He wanted to change this.

In 1982 Robert was given a national award called the MacArthur Foundation Genius award. The award was for Robert's civil rights work in Mississippi. He used the money from this award to help him fund his new civil rights project.

A new kind of work

Robert believed math was an important skill. He made his children do math problems at home every day. This math was in addition to the math they did at school. But his daughter, Maisha, thought that was too much work. She said she did not want to do math both at home and at school.

Robert asked Maisha's eighth-grade teacher if he could come to school to teach Maisha math. The math he would teach was harder than what her class was learning. Three other students wanted to join them. Robert helped the students do **algebra.** Algebra is a type of math in which letters are used to represent unknown numbers. Most students take algebra in the ninth grade. Robert and his students sat in a corner of the classroom. They had algebra lessons while the rest of the class did eighth-grade math.

With Robert's help, Maisha and the other students learned algebra. That spring, they became the first students at their school to pass the Cambridge city math test. This meant they qualified to take honors math and science courses in high school. Students who had not passed the test could not take these classes.

Robert wanted every student to study algebra. In 1982, he created a program called the Algebra Project to help all students.

A student works out a math problem on the chalkboard. Robert created the Algebra Project to help all students pass the city math test.

The Algebra Project

The Algebra Project was a new kind of **civil rights** project. Many African-American students were in easy math classes. So were poor white students and students of other races. Robert believed that these students were as smart as the students in regular math classes. He believed that every student could learn algebra and pass the city math test. Then they would be able to take the high school classes they needed to prepare for college.

Robert thought that the students could learn math if it were taught in an interesting way. He also thought the students could learn math if they believed they could. Robert tried to relate math to the students' lives. He created a math lesson using African drumming and another using rap songs. He took the students on field trips. They tried to discover how everyday math works in daily life.

Now Robert and other **volunteers** visited area schools and gave special math lessons. They taught teachers and parents, too. Teachers working with the Algebra Project were not teachers in the traditional sense. Teachers helped students figure out the answers on their own. They were just there to help. That way students could feel proud because they did the work themselves.

Parents came to school on Saturdays. They learned the algebra that they had not learned in school when they were younger. Now, they would stop thinking math was too hard, and they could help their children with homework.

In the Algebra Project, successful people were **role models** for the students. A role model is an older person whom a younger person can look up to. The role models were important. They helped students see that other people could do math. The role models were tutors who helped students with their lessons. They went to schools and gave speeches. They made it seem "cool" to be good in math. This helped the students believe in themselves.

Actor Danny Glover, shown here in January of 2003, was one of the volunteer tutors for Robert's Algebra Project.

Some role models were African Americans who went to college and had good jobs. Some were famous. Actor Danny Glover was an Algebra Project role model. All of these role models were volunteers.

Much of Robert's family still works with the Algebra Project. Janet works to gain funding for the program. His children are involved as well. Maisha is now in charge of training math teachers. His sons, Omowale and Taba, started the Young People's Project, or YPP. This is a tutoring branch of the Algebra Project.

Through the Algebra Project, Moses helps minority and poor students learn algebra. He believes that if students take high school classes that prepare them for college, more students will go to college.

Older students share their math skills with new students. Sometimes the YPP travels to schools. They perform rap songs to teach kids math.

Today, the Algebra Project is in 28 school districts across the United States. Teachers and volunteers help about 40,000 students every year learn math. They have summer camps and after-school math clubs. Robert did not forget about the poor African

Americans in Mississippi. The Southern Initiative of the Algebra Project brings algebra lessons to poor schools in southern states, including Mississippi.

Awards for his work

Robert Moses has received many awards for helping others. In 1994 Robert was given an award from *Essence* magazine. He got another award in 2000 from the Heinz Family Foundation. In 2001 he received the Nation/Puffin Prize for Creative Citizenship. In 2002 he received two awards. One was the Mary Chase Award for American Democracy. The other award was the James Conant Bryant Award for the Education Commission of the States. In 2000 the government of Mississippi declared May 2–3 Bob Moses Day for his work with **civil rights.**

Robert is still a quiet leader. He did not give a long speech when he accepted his *Essence* award. Instead, he told his students to come onto the stage. The students performed a math rap song. They proved how much Robert had taught them.

He has told students, "I can't make you take algebra, but this is why you want to. Algebra opens the door to college preparation. You may not go to college, but if you don't go it should not be because you haven't prepared yourself to go."

Glossary

algebra type of math that uses letters and numbers in the problems

civil rights individual rights that all members of a society have to freedom and equal treatment under the law

Civil Rights Era period of time (1955–1965) when people worked actively for freedom and equal treatment for African Americans in the United States. Also known as the Civil Rights Movement.

convention large gathering of people who have the same interests. Conventions can last for several days, and they consist of many meetings.

Democratic Party one of the two main groups in the United States that campaigns for control of the government

discrimination unfair behavior toward others based on differences in age, race, or gender

equal rights treatment of people so that they have the same opportunities and the same legal rights, no matter what their race or gender

Great Depression worldwide business slump of the 1930s. Many people lost their jobs and homes during this time.

National Association for the Advancement of Colored People (NAACP) national group founded in 1909 that works for equal rights for African Americans

nonviolent avoiding violence; peaceful

philosophy study of a person's ideas about how life should be lived

picket line line of people protesting something they do not like; the people in the picket line often hold signs.

protest event in which people join together to show they are against something

register to enter something on an official list

role model person who acts as an example for someone else

scholarship award that pays for someone to go to school

segregate keep separate, or keep people or things apart from the main group

segregation act or practice of keeping people or groups apart. Segregation laws kept blacks and whites separated from each other.

sit-in protest action in which a group of people sit in an area and refuse to move until their requests are heard

Student Nonviolent Coordinating Committee (SNCC) national group of students that worked to gain equal rights for African Americans

volunteer to offer to do a job, usually without pay, in order to help someone or learn something

Timeline

1935: Robert Parris Moses is born in Harlem, New York.

1948: Robert begins high school in New York.

1952: Robert wins a scholarship to Hamilton College in New York.

1956: Robert receives a Bachelor of Arts degree from Hamilton College. In the fall, he begins school at Harvard University in Cambridge, Massachusetts.

1957: Robert receives his Masters degree in **Philosophy** from Harvard.

1958: Robert's mother dies. Robert begins teaching math at Horace Mann High School.

1960: Robert Goes to Mississippi for the first time as a **SNCC volunteer**.

1961: Robert helps the first African-American people **register** to vote in Amite County, Mississippi.

Robert teaches high school students at **Nonviolent** High School.

1963: Robert and other SNCC volunteers are shot at while driving.

Jimmy Travis is shot and injured.

1963: Robert works on the Freedom Vote.

1964: Robert works on Freedom Summer.

1969: Robert and his family move to Tanzania. He teaches math there.

1976: Robert Returns to the United States and begins doctorate degree studies at Harvard.

1982: Volunteers at his daughter's school to help with math. He receives the MacArthur Foundation Genius grant.

1989: The first Algebra Project teachers are trained.

1992: The Southern Initiative of Algebra Project begins.

Further Information

Further reading

Altman, Susan. *Extraordinary African-Americans*: From Colonial to Contemporary Times. New York: Children's Press, 2001.

Meltzer, Milton. *There Comes a Time: The Struggle for Civil Rights.* New York: Random House, 2001.

Truck, Mary. *The Civil Rights Movement for Kids: A History with 21 Activities.* Chicago: Chicago Review Press, 2000.

Weber, Michael. *The African-American Civil Rights Movement.* Chicago: Raintree, 2001.

Addresses

The Algebra Project
National Headquarters
99 Bishop Allen Drive
Cambridge, MA 02139
Write here for more information about the Algebra Project.

Medgar Evers Museum
332 Margaret West Alexander Drive
Jackson, MS 39213
Write here with your questions about the civil rights leader Medgar Evers.

National Association for the Advancement of Colored People
4805 Mount Hope Drive
Baltimore, MD 21215
Write to learn more about the NAACP.

Southern Christian Leadership Conference (SCLC)
PO Box 89128
Atlanta, GA 30312
Write here to learn more about the SCLC.

Index